Eye UNLOCKED

Eye Unlocked

Poems, Short Stories and Illustrations

Linda M. Washington

PUBLICATIONS GROUP, INC.

Silver Spring

Published in the United States by
Beckham Publications Group, Inc.
P.O. Box 4066, Silver Spring, MD 20914

ISBN: 978-0-9823876-4-1

Contents

Part 3: Mystery Journeys

Part 4: Relationships and Romances

Acknowledgments

Thanks to my sons, Andrew Kenneth McDermon, Jr. and Jonathan Berry, for their loving support, which inspired me to achieve my lifetime goal.

I searched deep inside my soul to set higher goals. I only ask my two sons to follow their goals.

To my mother, Mrs. Mary Magdalene Washington, who raised us single-handedly and gave us advice on life's opportunities. She asked us to push beyond our expectations and limitations to better our lives.

Thanks to my sister, Mrs. Joann Harley-Blackwell, may she rest in peace.

To Mrs. Juanita M. George, Mrs. Clara S. Washington, Mrs. Mary M. Barton, and Shirley Washington, for their inspiring conversations.

Thanks to my brothers, Mr. Crosby F. Washington, Jr., Mr. Paul F. Washington, Mr. Carl T. Washington, and Douglas B. Washington, for their strength and encouraging words. Also, I'd like to mention the role model figures my brothers played without our dad.

I acknowledge my father, the late Mr. Cosby F. Washington, Sr., and may he rest in peace.

Thanks to special friends, Mrs. Dorothy Coleman, Mrs. Jewel Spencer-Bye, and Mrs. Janice Evans, for their inspiring words of encouragement.

Thanks to Mr. Roger James, the inspiring artist behind all the artwork throughout the book, and to me, for masterminding the art displayed throughout the book.

Thanks to everyone who supported my dream of creating the book, *Eye Unlocked*.

PART 1

Acts of Kindness

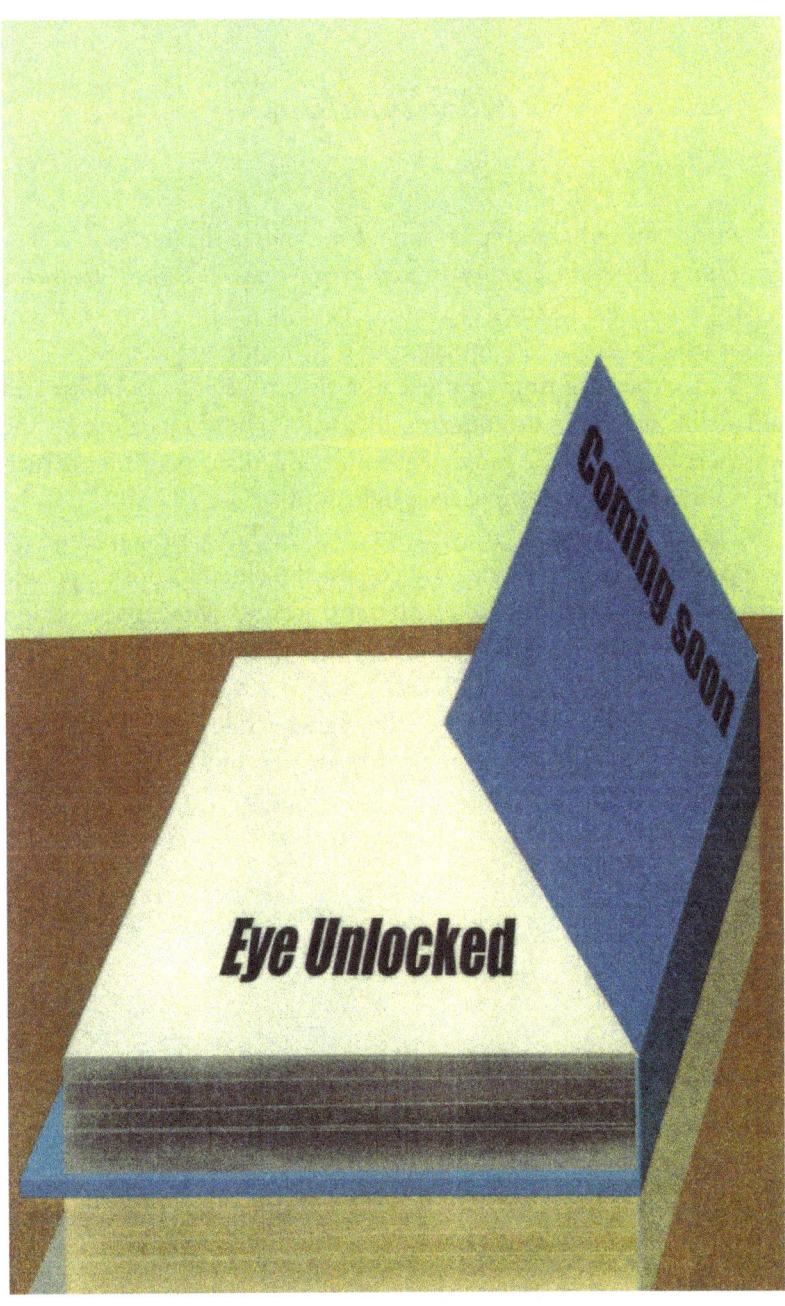

Moonlighting

I once moonlighted, part time, for a movie theater.

Hurry! Hurry! Come on in and get in line. As soon as the doors open, find a seat. I stayed up late last night reading a story. Right about now, I just need a moment of down time to feel alive.

I am expecting time to move at a slow pace. The popcorn and soft drink machines are buzzing like bees. The doors close so the watchers can enjoy the movie without being disturbed. Lights turn off. Only the large movie screen light is on.

I heard moviegoers enjoying themselves. Then, time to close up and prepare for another day. Once past the cinema's doors, people chatted and debated about different scenes. Moviegoers stood against the walls, waiting to exit the crowded doors. Sometimes, I would stay around and help clean up.

I got paid cash at the end of the night. While helping clean up, I thought about writing a book. I heard that an interesting story stimulates a reader's brain.

So, readers . . . get ready to read my book, *Eye Unlocked*!

Don't Forget

Come take me out tonight, then wake me in the morning.

Tell me that you love me, too, and then kiss away the pain.

Hold my hand and say you love me every day.

And, if I shall die, before I wake,

Kiss me and say *goodbye*.

1901-2011
Mrs. Flower

Flowers

Tulips, roses, daisies and all

Growing and growing so beautiful and defined.

Fresh when cut and wither at times.

They all have their means,

For flowers will die when nobody thinks,

A silly old flower could have meant nothing.

Stop, look and admire the existence that nature bore,

And realize that there has never been a soul,

Buried beneath the blooms.

Genesis—My Version

Turning forty is a blessing. Did you know? God fasted for forty days and forty nights?

Then he created Earth. Then man. He then pierced man's side to remove a rib. God used that rib to create the most wonderful creature in this world: Woman.

Now forty and haven't wrinkled a bit.

You're looking finer then a forty-year-old bottle of wine.

Body so well-preserved, almost like back in the Egyptian days, as if placed in white sheets to remain pure.

I watch you eat products of the Earth, like back in biblical times.

I adore the *Book of Genesis*, because it fits you well.

I'm glad I met someone as special as you, one in a million of sands here on Earth.

I'm glad we are friends and share a common bond, which we both call a son.

Therefore, I give you something special from Eden.

I will need to summon my ancient lamp to bring your biblical gift.

Maybe something authentic, pleasant, earthly, or from the Garden of Eden which symbolizes the beauty of life.

Maybe special flowers from brush Eve used to cover her body after she discovered nudity? I've decided: "Forty Flowers for each year here on Earth."

God and I

I have only known you for a short time.

I have only spent days, evenings, and nights with you for a short time.

I enjoy your company and listening to your concerns.

I understand your desire to stand tall and strong.

Tall and strong does not mean always alone.

I am right here, as a friend, to see you succeed.

I am a good provider for troubled minds.

I am a good listener and only intercede when you have finished your thoughts.

You do not always have to put people before yourself.

People will be around until God comes down and take us away to Judgment Day.

Focus on yourself, and your health, and remember you are a precious seed.

You are not here on Earth to carry the full responsibility of another.

That is God's job and God knows His job well.

I need you to relax.

I'll summon God to help you stand tall.

AII you need to do is shut off the acoustic valve.

And God will speak to your heart.

Hate, Love and Help

I am a spirit wearing a light-skinned coat. My spirit will not allow me to detest. My ideology steers me out the pathway of mischief. I have principles. I cannot see myself being cruel to mankind. I dare to swallow up hate.

I see myself as an assistance provider.

And I like helping people whose needs are just as important as mine.

So, I dare choose neither hate nor cruelty.

I fell in love with another four-letter word

HELP.

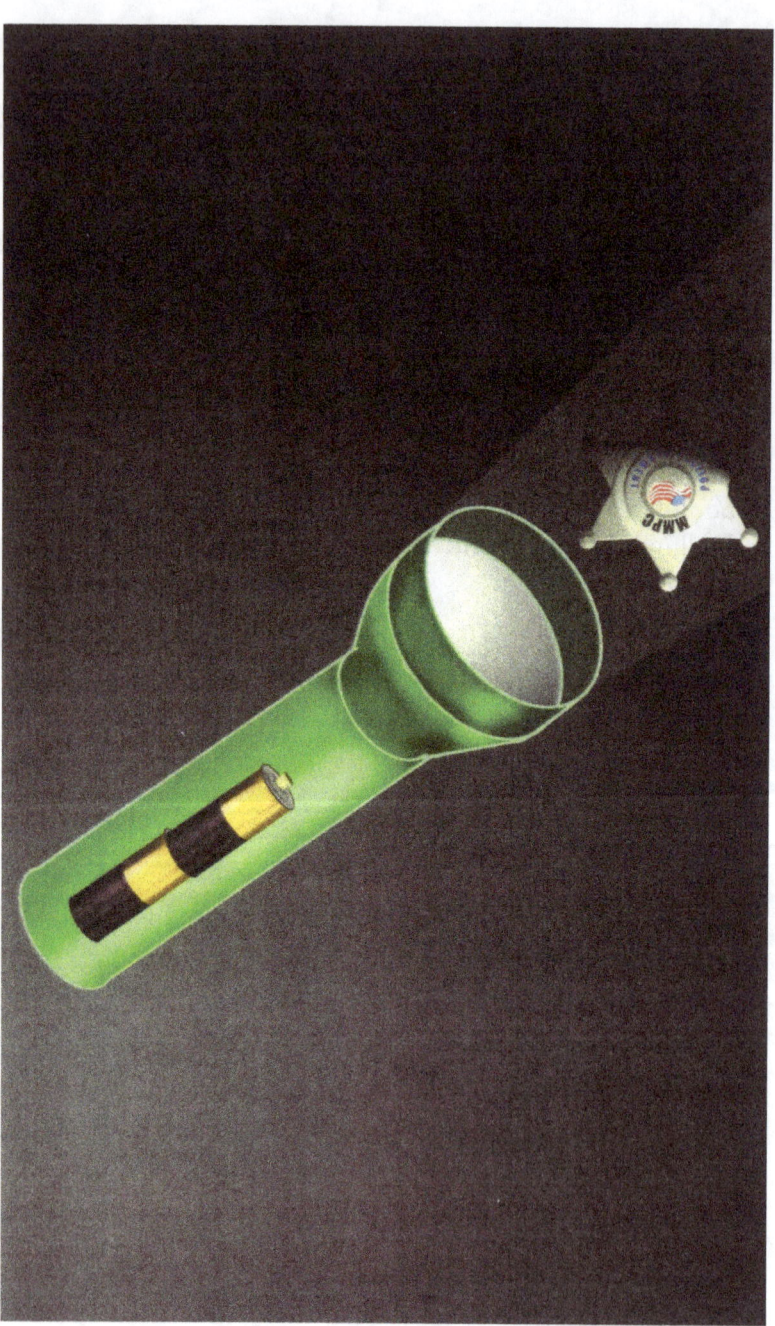

Let There Be Light

A gift from a prudent police officer, who thinks of your safety, day, evening and especially midnight,

I purchased you a flashlight.

I invested in Duracell batteries, because they take a licking and keep on going and going.

This flashlight has magical powers, especially from me and my partner, "God."

So, whenever you are sitting in your scout car and feel puzzled by a problem,

I want you to click on your flashlight,

Then aim it at a star and wish for your solution.

God will dim the light on your flashlight three times,

To let you know He understands and He is with you every step of the way.

If, by chance, your flashlight disappears one day, He will light up an entire crime scene,

And make sure you, and any fellow officers around you, are safe.

Doesn't matter whether the officers are in dark blue uniforms, white shirts, or plain clothes.

I asked God for that very special effort before I even decided to purchase your flashlight.

Keep in mind, quality items sometimes disappear in this department.

I don't want anything to happen to you, just because someone else wanted to see the light differently.

Out of Birthday Comes Art

I decided to do art for your birthday, so I searched the Internet for a brilliant artist of your liking.

There were many famous works by artists like Pablo Picasso, Vincent van Gough, Leonardo da Vinci, Claude Monet, Michelangelo, Rembrandt, and Salvador Dali, but I decided to step out on faith and went with a local artist by the name of

Roger James

And on that note, I present you with a gift of gratitude, for being an exceptional mother.

Art

There is nothing more precious in this world than a child.

He draws a school picture that made my heart skip a beat and takes my breath away.

Art

Art work so authentic, it's not sold in the stores or galleries.

Art

Artists often say, "A picture is worth a thousand words."

Art

I made it clear to my artist that I wanted only clarity.

Art

And the truth of this picture is

Art

The image of the boy inside the picture transforms as he grows into adulthood outside the picture frame.

The drawing of boy will not change or decrease in value.

Happy Birthday!

The Final Call

He heard a spiritual voice, and within moments, Officer A.S. was chosen and highly recommended, to come into the lord's place. Highly recommended, I do say so myself. He was chosen because his smile was like that of a cheerful missionary. He had the endowment to work hard; his spirit kept him always on call. Officer A.S's family, friends, and members of the police department are on stand-by. God called him to another working environment, much safer than here on Earth. He did rest up for a while before starting on his journey. He could not leave his co-workers, family, and friends without giving them more time to visit and stay.

He lay still, his mind wandering among the clouds. He was curious if traffic jams in heaven would be anything like the ones he saw at the hospital. He knew this was his final time here on Earth. He envisioned his wife's hands tight against his own as he talked in a mute, spiritual voice. He knew his wife could understand. He would walk with her again, side by side, in the house of the lord— forever and ever, amen.

A voice said, "see the light." Eyes opened as a bright light appeared; suddenly, everyone in the hospital vanished.

The moment was sudden, without him saying his final words. And, whenever an officer loses his life at the call of an assignment, we honor that officer as "highly recommended."

The final call.

Wives' Father's Day Tribute

Ladies, let's do our husband a favor.

Let's take him out to the ball game.

Then feed him many peanuts and Cracker Jacks.

Then take him home for a special delight.

Ask him to bare the body to enjoy the flight.

Then heat some baby oil to rub the body right.

Use your finger tips to rub up and down his spine.

Until the oil saturates.

Then participate by opening your mouth to taste the juices.

They say that the tongue absorbs liquid faster than anything else.

Make sure you have a towel on hand to wipe away any extra juices once you're satisfied.

Once satisfied, wrap him up in a warm blanket and tuck him in bed.

And give him a juicy kiss.

And tell him,

You will always love him.

Coming from a positive female figure,

Mrs. Wife.

PART 2

Life's Adversities

A Talking Photo

I am a young black boy inside a frame

dressed in black and white print

surrounded by borders

showing my true colors

I cross my arms to put myself in a comfortable position.

I wear my hair natural, like wool.

I hold my head straight up.

As I square off with the camera lens.

I must say, I'm self-assured and making a statement.

I'm a young black boy indeed.

And, now, my photo is in all store windows and galleries.

I see both of my parents looking proud as African-American Native.

And that is why I must stay true to the cause.

Hence I posed for the photo to remind myself, as a young black boy, art is *making a statement.*

Being a Woman

When a woman laughs and smiles, it brightens the day.

When a woman cries, she saves no tears.

She bows down in silence and shuts off all sounds.

Her thoughts wander but her soul remains steadfast

rooted to the ground for the very people she loves.

She carries the spirit of home and lights up every dark room.

A woman she may be, soft as marshmallow inside

But when faced with rough times

She hardens like a rock.

Let's Ask God

Each person has his own character.

A star on their own world.

A tender reality never unarmed.

With love, grace, and those heavenly gifts God has planned for that person's destiny.

Sometimes a person has to reap what he sows.

And sometimes the opposite,

A person refuses to sow.

Yet, whatever a person has opted, God has the last say.

Letter to "Way"

Hello Way,

I received your letter today. Settled me in a state of tranquility. I know why Maya Angelou wrote, "Why do the caged birds sing?" The bird trapped in a cage, not able to move about freely. No truth like the American Airlines motto "You are free to move about the plane." Yet, the bird cries a trilling sound inside the cage, heard by his family members outside the wall. What family member would not have a hard time shutting out the painful cries which echo miles away? No outlet to free the soul, except the space between solid steel bars. He questions *why would any human being steal my soul?* Way, I can relate to the line in your letter about rage. Knowing your inner soul is like the caged bird, trapped in a cell hole, surrounded by mind-crippling warriors, all trying to survive a game called life.

Like Nelson Mandela, incarcerated for twenty-eight years in a South African prison. His living conditions were excruciating; he prepared himself by quieting the mind, body, and soul every day, on a concrete floor. He refused to be hog washed by people of the same color. He knew poverty kept them from assimilating intellectual knowledge. He knew the guards, governed by dictatorship, were left spiritless; they were considered lost souls. Mandela's punishment was mandatory hard labor for life. Mandela, in his right frame of mind, isolated evil thoughts and focused on home.

Like Dorothy in the Wizard of Oz; she clicked her high heels three times and ended up back home in Kansas.

Mandela knew the journey, one day, would bring release.

Mandela kept hope alive, with the right frame of mind, and made it home to become President of South Africa.

Horses can be led to the water, but you can't make them drink. Live for hope, Way. What brings us happiness is not the destination, but the journey. Throw out the trash inside your mind, Way.

Here are three rules of life. I learned from a movie, *Paradox*, that life is a mystery; don't waste time trying to figure it out. Humor: keep a sense of humor, especially about yourself; it is the strength that overcomes. Changes: know that nothing stays the same. Also remember that, for every action, there are results. Way, I close with my thoughts with a quote from Mrs. Whitney Houston, "I'll always love you."

Me

"*Please do not close and shut me down,*" said me.

"*Please do not frown and look down on me,*" said me.

"*Please do not judge me, I have not told you about me,*" said me.

"*Please don't underestimate me, "'cause I know me,'*" said me

Love me for I am, a simple being me, a part of song that describe what the *me* wanted.

Respect/Judge me after knowing the simple *me*.

Mental-Physical Imbalance

Have you ever wanted something and realized you were cutting your own throat?

Have you ever thought about changing your mental and physical self-being?

Have you ever focused on going to the mountain top

to rid yourself of a mental thing and conquer a defeat called fear?

Have you ever sat down by a clear, blue river, running briskly,

and wondered, what keeps it clean? Physical or mental?

Have you ever looked in the mirror and asked yourself, who am I? Physical or mental?

To answer those questions, you must exercise your mental mind.

And focus on your dreams.

And tell yourself, "You are somebody."

And even when you think it cannot get any worse.

Spare yourself: do not consider being a cutthroat.

Remind yourself: life has places worth admiring.

And know life, sometimes, throws us curve balls.

You can miss out, if your mind kept on flying endlessly and with no direction.

So stay in shape, tone yourself physically and mentally at all times

Start exercising your mind by being active, productive, and most importantly, stably balanced.

Slavery

Work and live knowing how to play.

Work and know pay.

Working and not knowing why, your working was insane.

Chain us up, for we will not run.

Punish us, for we will not understand.

And free us, for our time is here.

Work and no play will go our way.

Work and pay we do say.

Working and not knowing: why, we're working insane.

Punish us no more, 'cause we've finally awakened.

Our ancestors explained: the treatment we've taken.

Now, I understand why work was so hard, back in the centuries.

Those people back then on the selection panel, beyond my comprehension, who made them God?

Steps

Step up

Step down

Step forward

Step back

Step aside, but don't

Step completely out of sight.

Stop

(aaa)

audio, activation, accidents

Stop AAA

I'm a street cyclist, meaning, I ride the streets. I'm gifted with a pair of heavy-duty legs. I have two lovers. Their names are Mr. Raleigh and Mr. Schwinn.

I ride them both everywhere. I see Mr. Winter is fading away.

And I see Mr. Spring coming to play.

I am going to ride Raleigh first. I like how he feels.

When I ride, I dress up or dress down.

I wear my biker's gloves, helmet and bike shoes.

And I ride around town.

I drink plenty of OJ for the vitamin C.

Before I journey outside the house, I pack away Mr. Deer Park.

I sip while I ride. I strap my iPod on my side. I wrap my entire ear lobes with headphones to keep the music from getting away. I shut off all natural sounds and street noise.

I ride, like Mr. Crow, flying in and out of traffic. I often disobey the traffic laws.

I ride down one-way streets. I rode up on a chalk silhouette, lying in the street. I see a cyclist, struck by a vehicle. The bike's frame, twisted like a pretzel.

Headphones torn apart, lying in the street. The cord to the iPod, still attached to the silhouette. I suddenly detached my sound for silence. A voice gave me a notion.

You should design a billboard for triple A.

It would say: Stop AAA from occurring; stop Audio Activation Accidents!

White Causes Adversities

When snow, sugar, salt and cocaine first hit the streets, they're all untainted.

Whether fallen from the sky or misused in the body.

The color white can cause adversities.

Weather storm advisers predict that ten inches of snow could cause our city to panic and stagnate people's movements.

Doctor White said, "Overindulge in sweets, diagnosis diabetes."

Doctor White said, "Overload on salt, diagnosis high blood pressure."

Doctor White said, "Crystal rock, so potent, diagnosis death."

That's cocaine, nothing else common there, but the color (white).

Simply nerve-wracking; it's the number one "killer" and "killed for."

I've watched people self-destruct on these products.

They either inject, or snort, the white poisonous products into their bodies

Street policy says, "no customer sampling the product, until the seller has left your sight."

Some customers are already high, before purchasing the dirty white powder. Their taste buds are so numb, they wouldn't know; it could be baby powder, salt, crystal, sugar, or vitamins.

Somewhat different from uptown/downtown Beverly Hills, California, where the living conditions are exceptional, captivating.

We enjoy the fun by just kicking back. You have your own new drug

paraphernalia supply. No more sharing needles, just snorted me up.

The most dramatic irony is that such a dangerous white powder can permeate a neighborhood of color so easily, killing the person.

Yes, I know these products are harmful to your health. No, I am not Doctor White.

See, I enjoy the snow.

Snow purifies the air, slows the traffic down, and keeps my brothers and sisters off the street for a couple of days. Good luck with the color white. When I see white, it worries me, because I know it must get dirty

It always does.

PART 3

Mystery Journeys

An Illusion of a Christmas Robbery

It was the night before Christmas and I was out of the house. I went cruising to Citibank in Rockville, Maryland, to scope out the bank.

When out the front door, I saw a woman, wearing a long-length red coat and a Santa Claus hat, a sack of money in one hand, briefcase in the other.

I came up behind her, quicker than a flash, dressed like Santa Claus and armed with a candy cane. I stuck the candy cane in the center of her back. Said, "Tis the season to be jolly! Give up the loot for my darling."

The manager panicked and started to sing, "Oh come thee old faithful," before dropping the loot. I picked up the loot. Then thanked the manager by wishing her a Merry Christmas and safer New Year.

I glanced all around, to see a red and white car with flashing signal lights, my getaway car. I jumped into the car and shouted out loud, "Now dash away, dash away, and dash away home."

Eye Unlocked

Empathy kept me inside

You had the key, God, and let me outside,

Even when I had doubts, and

Underestimated my progression. You said,

Never again will I deceive you.

Your lifetime blessing,

An opportunity to succeed.

Challenge yourself,

Keep focused, and

Set in your mind in becoming the # 1 seller and

Declare publishing rights for your book,

Eye Unlocked.

I Am a Story Stalker

I am a nighttime, early morning, story stalker. I travel the streets of Southeast Washington, D.C., in the earliest hours of the morning, looking for stories from sunset to sunrise. I visit all of my familiar childhood and adulthood spots.

I reminisce about going back to my old school. I visit many churches. An empty lot where once sat my childhood house. I also visit Elizabeth. I meant Saint Elizabeth Hospital (mental Institution), my secret place away from home. My last stop, before I settle down to go home: Mr. Lincoln Cemetery, a graveyard site, and my last home here on Earth, looking for stories.

I am a story stalker.

I am now working the graveyard shift at DC Superior Court. My title, classified by the public as blue coat officer. The location is District of Columbia Superior Courthouse. The building was built back in 1979. I perform various duty assignments on the graveyard shift. The building interior makeup consists of about 120 court rooms, nurse's station, information booth, and more. There are employees occupying pre-trial services, twenty-four seven. The court, too, offers night filing services to the public and attorneys.

As a Court Security Officer, one of my duties is to check the building in its entirety. Give special attention to the judge's chamber, located behind the corridor's center interior hallway. The judge's chambers are off limits to the public and security personnel. Security personnel do have access to the corridors. Some floors have corridors that run one-third of a mile in length. When I look down the hallway, I envision, in my mind, running a race. I say, "On your marks, get set, ready, go." And I take off down the stretch. I immediately get a mental high. I break out in a sweat. My blue coat, pants, shirt, all feel damp, and my forehead is sweating profusely.

I experience a terrific hot flash watching the stretch. Yet, I never make a motion.

Afterward, I walk the third of a mile length to clear my mind, and then, a theological moment pops up. The judge's chambers resembles the pathway in the Bible. The chambers on both sides of the corridors have many rooms.

St. John, Chapter 14.2: *in my father's house are many mansions: if it were not so, I would not have said so. I go to prepare a place for you.* When I patrol the hallways, on many occasions, I hear those words reverberating in my mind. I then picture the entire area. Two patios, side windows, center corridors by the exit doors. The judges' elevators doors are bronze and gold. Inside the elevators, bronze-colored rails, cherry wooden panels, and illuminated lights in the ceiling. The walls are painted a brilliant yellow, brightening the earthly green borders. I know my sixth sense has kicked into gear; my workplace is safe.

I am a story stalker

I often work construction overtime on one of my days off. My days off are Wednesday and Thursday nights. The construction company's hours vary, depending on the company. I love getting off that early in the morning.

I drive to the 7-11 off South Capitol Street S.W., in Washington, DC. I purchase a large coffee. Then, I proceed across the South Capitol Street Bridge into Southeast Washington, DC. I am going sightseeing. My first stomping ground is Second Street, right off Atlantic Street, Southeast. I go to the park area there, to see a display of deer galloping during early morning darkness. I see, in someone's front yard, a buck eating a yellow-colored grass. I pull my truck over and stalk the deer for a while. He is unaware of my presence and continues to eat. Once I am through sightseeing, I proceed to the corner of South Capitol Street, off Second Street. My church sits on the hilltop: Covenant Baptist Church. I usually go there to read the bulletin. I notice the light bulbs, in the program bulletin, have burned out. I can't read a lesson or receive a message. So, I say a little prayer for myself and my family.

I am still lurking in the early morning darkness. I drive to Ballou High School, located at Fourth and Trenton Street, Southeast, Washington, D.C., my old high school.

Back in 1979, I recall applying to the Metropolitan Police Department. Two years had gone by before I received a call from a recruiter asking if I was still interested. I accepted the job. I had only two months to shape up, from October 1981 to December 14, 1981.

I revisited Ballou High School's track and field and trained myself. I ran hard, every day, for weeks. I watched our school mascot, displayed on the score board. Go Knights! Go Knights! I thought about being a horse for two months; I transformed my mindset to believe I was a horse, and pushed beyond my aches and pains. The academy was only two months away. I've made the journey now, and retired.

I recently cruised around Ballou High School; I noticed the renovation for the summer of 2013 had already begun. The football field, which surrounds the track and field, was already fenced off and demolition had started. Now I must run the streets of the city to get a meaningful workout.

I am a story stalker.

Saint Elizabeth Hospital was one of my memorable workout spots, too. I once worked on the grounds of the facilities. As I look around, wandered my eyes all over the place, and thought to myself, this place was an endless river. There were acres and acres of beautiful landscaping which ran for miles with no familiar pattern.

And it ran east and west, only separated by walls, fences, or the open underground tunnel connecting the east and west sides.

I rode my bike all around the grounds. I even ran the grounds with my Walkman in my ears, enjoying the music. I would sing loud once in a while. And, I felt myself being right at home. So when I heard sounds of a patient screaming and shouting, that was the norm.

The facilities had their own movie theater, cafeterias, stores, a main hospital, a jail, a fire department, police security personnel, and more. I do say, the main attraction was the point which oversees downtown Washington. I loved that picturesque scene.

Even the patients enjoyed their space around the point. I felt at home. Yet, I had access to the East grounds, by using my retired police badge. I no longer had access to west grounds, since Homeland Security now requires a top secret clearance. I traveled on the east side of the grounds. I saw the tunnel, leading to the west side, bricked off. I doubted if the patients from each side ever had a fight on the other. Now all my spots of secrecy must be written in a story. Farewell, Elizabeth.

I am a story stalker.

Good morning, Mr. Lincoln's Cemetery.

I arrived at Lincoln Cemetery during business hours. I pulled on the door, using caution. I know, on a windy day, pulling on the tailor's door handle could cost you your life. I recall, on a windy day, being blown to the rear of the tailor's after opening the door. My thoughts were to fly out the back window. I thought I might land near a burial site. Now, when I opened the door, I proceeded with caution. I often look for caution signs. Nevertheless, I gripped the door handle tightly so as not to fly away.

The grounds upkeep was, indeed, in need of some tender loving landscape. I saw gravesites so deep in the dumps, they were missing in action. Similar to families who have loved ones buried at Lincoln: how poorly kept, the grounds. Perhaps these families never visit their loved ones' gravesites to see. Perhaps there are bodies buried together, as one. Yet, I invested in four deadly spots myself.

My mother likes the hilltop view. We decided to invest in four spots on the hilltop. The hilltop view is like a step closer to heaven. The hilltop song is "Go tell it on the mountain that Jesus Christ was born."

Sir, where the tailor settles, build a house and show some class. l also suggest you invest in a "Welcome" mat. And, I recommend you give the tailor to the homeless as a starter home. Sir, spend your money for *goodness* sake.

I Commute on Mute

The hustle and bustle of my subway morning commutes. The Southern Avenue Metro Station, located at 1911 Southern Avenue, Temple Hills, Maryland, is directly across the street from my residence. The station opens early at 5:00 am. When I arrive at the station, I see Metro Transit uniformed personnel and speak. I look to my right-hand side and notice several Metro Fare machines about 20 feet away from me.

These machines are available to help customers. I gain access through the gates by touching my plastic Metro fare card against the Metro logo. Once I pass through the gates, I like to play a game called "Who Is Aware of Their Surroundings?" There is an elevator on site, equipped with a 4500 lbs. capacity sign, jammed with commuters. They are going down to the platform to await the arrival of the train. I always walk down the stairs; just that little bit of exercise starts my day. While proceeding downstairs, I immediately focus my attention on the overhead destination directories. These directories display the arrival time of each train. I position myself in one of the station's seven bay booths. I notice there are large area and zone maps, framed in Plexiglas, for passengers to read. Attached to the concrete walls on both sides of the tracks are several signs. The signs show the stations' line destinations and transfer stops. There are surveillance cameras mounted on the ceilings.

Pay telephones are encircled by individual cubicles and trash receptacles. Sealed circle lights are embedded in the concrete platform. They flash to show when the train is arriving.

Once the train arrives, people bunch up tightly and hurry aboard to get a seat. Sometimes, there are no seats available: standing room only. When this occurs, I go to the rear, close to the conductor's booth. The area makes you feel like you're trapped in a sea of people with no door out. Once the train is ready for traveling, the conductor announces, "Stand clear of the doors, the doors are closing." Sometimes the conductors have to repeat themselves; "Stand clear of the doors, the doors are closing."

I prepare myself for a comfortable stand-up ride. I know there are five more stops before I reach my destination, and Anacostia Station is the second stop.

This is where we meet a large mass of people boarding the train. We become so packed together that our bodies feel connected by hip, neck, and backside. We remain this way until we leave each other. Sometimes we are so close that we become helpless, in an intimate fashion, not by design.

Sometimes there are sounds of unidentified music in your ears from one stop to the next. Sometimes there are noises of chattering, almost like someone is speaking in tongues.

I begin to focus on the surrounding sounds. Then, here come the small children. Book bags strapped on their shoulders, hands so tiny; they reach the safety rails. When the train is in motion, I sometimes witness the children grabbing onto someone's ass to keep from falling.

These behaviors attract a lot of attention from women, forcing the adults to participate in the "grab a child" program. You want to hold on to them to ensure they don't fall. You can do that, or offer them a seat.

I start to see the men, comfortable in seats. Some of the guys are sleeping; some listening to music with headphones; some reading the newspaper, and some are sightseeing. The guys with manners immediately surrender their seats. Then there are the men who are properly blindfolded to liberal women and bratty children. I have been wandering my eyes all over the place. Observing the men in the surroundings. How I define them, how I see them fit.

1. A cultured man who behaves with courtesy and thoughtfulness.
2. A man from a high social class, especially a man with an independent mindset.
3. A man who honors women first, realizing that, without women, there could be no him. This is modern day creation, not biblical days.

I believe that every able man, who abides by the above standards, should give up his seat to women and children.

I enjoy seeing these different situations. It's breathtaking to stand, or sit, and wonder about a person's mindset.

I commute on mute.

People on the train sometimes find themselves apologizing because of a certain circumstance.

This usually happens when the train is wobbling, then suddenly jerks. This causes people to deliver body blows to others, by mistake.

"Sorry," is the right term to use to apologize. Even the conductor announces an apology; "Sorry, the train will be moving momentarily; a train ahead."

I am almost at my destination, one more before L'Enfant Plaza. This is the transfer station from the green Line to the red Line, blue line, yellow line, and orange Line.

When the doors open, people disappear and seats become available. The conductor starts his routine announcement. "Stand clear of the doors. Doors are closing. Next stop, Archives Naval-Memorial." Finally here!

Before exiting the train, I see the seat color patterns match the train line's green, red, orange, blue and yellow. Now, what genius almost pulled that one over on "Who Is Aware of Their Surroundings?"

"Goodbye." I am on my merry way.

I gather my duffle bag off the floor and launch it onto my shoulder. I walk up a flight of stairs, through the pay gates, and onto the Metro elevator. I head across the street to Starbucks, located at 7th and E. Street Northwest, Washington, DC. I buy my favorite coffee; I like a large Caramel mocha with extra Caramel in soymilk, and hold the foam.

The irony is, "I commute on mute," but all the while, I'm mentally talking with myself.

Past

Let's check on the past. Let's look back over half a century ago. Let's tighten our eyelids and try to reminisce on the first touch, the first mumbled words, and the many cries of childhood. Our childhood upbringing, raised by a single mother or dad, meant a lot. Where having two parents meant more benefits. Whatever the case may have been, the love from any human adult during childhood meant the world.

Let's relive nursery school, grade school, middle school, high school and college. Let's incorporate wildlife experiences, emotional roller coaster rides, our first true love, and our worst nightmares. Let's recall the first love panicking moment. Let's wonder how we survived our first helpless tactic, which surrendered us speechless. Let's compare friends in the past to friends now.

Let's think about the first love. Let's think about the lover who nearly depleted us of life's fresh air. Who nearly took our breath away. Let's recall some vicious love cycles, where snap behaviors defined a cry for help. Passions, so deep for another, we lost focus on ourselves. The fixated behavior which kept us attached to each other. A remark made in a suicide relationship. If I can't have you, no one can.

Someone hurry! Call 911! Tell the operator this is an emergency. Marvin Gaye's hit song, "Sexual Healing," hit the nail right on the hammer. He said, "Help you to relieve your mind, makes you feel so fine." Let's hear life's songs because most songs describe everyday, life-given situations.

Here are a few examples. When you cheat; your thoughts are "only for one night. I will not tell a soul. No one needs to know." Let's flip-flop on the cheater. Let's adventure into an affair.

The song should go like, "If your love is my love, and my love is your love, we would live an eternity." How is this for the record? "There's no one who loves you like I do."

And when hurt and heart arouse in the same moment, we experience pain.

Let's call mother for guidance. She said, "Baby, I heard 'Love doesn't live here anymore'; it's just that simple." Okay! We go "on and cried my dear, and kiss away the pain." Then "pick up the pieces" and say "Love does not live here anymore."

There are love songs for all our lives' situations. Now, let's reminisce on old school oldies. The special theme song admired by most women. I am no more a little girl. I am a grown-up now. I am going to revisit the past, for the children's sake. Who remembers when we were children?

So, I release the past. And describe the past as "a distant road traveled back in time."

I also store my precious memories, back in time past, to share them, one day, with my granddaughter, or grandson, about their genuine dad, my child, my son, Andrew.

Stored in a mausoleum, in a folder, and sealed seven times, to be summoned by my father, only to be opened on my Judgment Day.

My Crystal Wish

I see this large circle following me.

Scientists call it the moon.

I call it my night knight and guiding armor.

It always protects me while I'm traveling to my destiny. The clouds part; around the corner, up the hill, to whatever destiny I go, it follows.

I've really become lackadaisical and extremely romantic when this circle forms to its fullest.

I feel elevated like on a skyscraper. Than suddenly I feel a emotional rise flowed my body through the clouds.

My eyes open extremely large and my pupils become dilated by the heavy glaze.

My sign is Cancer and the mood of my sign is breathtaking.

I see a pretty clear object in the sky following me around town.

It always reacts like a crystal ball for me.

The rays from the ball shine down into the water and show my reflection.

I toss a coin into the lake, then begin my wish: "Oh, crystal ball, oh crystal ball, grant my wish."

My Special Day

Every day is a special day

A day for growth

A day for happiness

A day to extend an open hand

A day to share wisdom

For every day is a fulfillment of all our desires

However, today is an exceptional day

Where life is unproblematic

Where love is a metaphor for a magnetizing disease

Where everyone ends up attracting that disease

And there is no cure

Never

A birthday gift, a "journal", a notepad with several phrases of wisdom.

"Write now."

I write words to touch others and inspire them to write.

I write to achieve my lifelong goals.

And quiz myself on adventure's goals.

Why would I travel the back road alone?

Someone may be lurking around to steal my joy.

Why would I sit in the back row of the auditorium?

I may miss out on valuable information to advance.

I play baseball. I always keep a good eye out for a tricky last pitch.

I only swing knowing someone could advance or score home.

Yet, I still doubt my writing skills.

My book will probably never be a number-one seller.

So, I pick up Mr. Webster, for clarity on *never*.

And negativity hit me in the face.

So, I refrain from using the word *never*.

And query it for testing purposes only.

A Talk with My Father

It was one cold, lonely night. I sat up in my bed, hands and arms crossed. I had to summon my father. My thought patterns were all jumbled up inside.

I needed father to check on my run-on sentences. Suddenly, without any warning, my mind went uncomprehending. I heard father say, "Write and I'll give you the words. They must remain clean, because I'm your salvation. There are so many like yourself, trying to seek eternal life.

"I have the gift of eternal life. You must come forward and receive the real I am. I will bring you no hardship. I am an exceptional father. Yet, people underestimate my authenticity.

"I own all corporations which provide services here on Earth. No credit card can purchase father. People, often unsure of themselves, call on special favors. Thinking they must appear right away. I have the power to do whatever I please.

"I'm not a destroyer; I have destroyed nations, leaving a few chosen people. I used water and fire. Yet, humans still feel the need to create weapons of mass destruction to destroy other nations.

"That is for their satisfaction, not the father's. I am nature, like the trees, flowers, fruit, and crops. I use water, soil, and plenty of tender, loving care."

Please, father, will you prove your powers? We know you can foresee all earthly life events before they occur.

Father acknowledges people's behaviors. Yet, he replied, "Be careful what you ask for, people. Remember, I gave my only son."

See, Father, that's really frightening, because I see my son as being so precious to me: like trees rooted from the soil.

Like a bright cloud admired in the clear blue sky. Like an endless river flowing and flowing upstream. Like the fruit grown on the trees: just right for harvest. Father, I never questioned your abilities to see what was forthcoming.

I just thank you, Lord Almighty Father, for someone as special as my son Andrew. Even if I thought Andrew could change the entire world with the gift of father. I would ask you, father, at this moment, for one favor: a life insurance policy, which reads:

"Mother and son will meet again in eternal life."

Thanks for the conversation father.

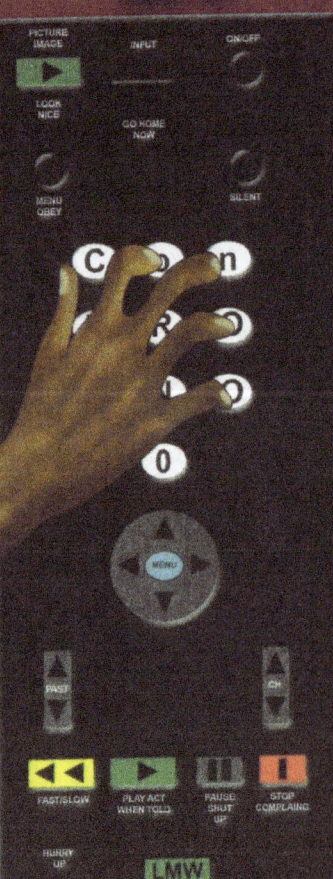

Selfish Soul

I need your body, mind and soul.

I need your body, in a delicious flavorful manner

I need your mind to think entertainment.

Quiet your mind, relax the body, and follow my soul.

I have come to inspire you to take an inner-body ride.

I am going to transform myself inside of you.

In one giant step, I can be loving you inside out.

I can feel your heart pulsating inside and out.

I want to touch your inner organs, causing your body to lose control.

I want to control you until you cannot tolerate the excitement anymore.

And you ask me out.

And you did; I heard a soft voice whisper in my ear, "release my body, mind, and soul."

I need to feel back in control of my own body, mind, and soul.

I came out to grant the wish.

I found myself lost.

I desperately felt on my own.

Suddenly, I realized my heart became weakened.

I entrusted in another human being for gratification purposes only.

I was selfish and knew better body, mind, and soul.

I wanted to be in control.

Because you allowed me control.

By no means do I want that much control over any human being.

There is only one exception to the rule; an infant who needs body, mind, and soul to enter to adulthood.

"Sir, You Are Not Alone"

On March 9, 1993, at 11:30 am, my intuition for writing this story propelled me to leave work. I went, nonstop, to my residence and removed DC's finest attire, my blue police uniform. I dressed down in a warm-up suit and pair of sneakers, trimmed in blue and white; my favorite color, blue. I love the color blue: it cultivates my mood swings.

My first destination: the grounds of Saint Elizabeth's Hospital, located on Martin Luther King Avenue in Southeast, Washington, DC. I proceeded to this area on the grounds, known to regular users as "the point." This area is simply breathtaking for lunch, relaxing or writing a story. It gives you wondrous views. You see places like the Washington Monument, National Airport, and Bolling Air Force Base. Then there's the Anacostia River, patterns of zigzag bridges, and transportation rapidly moving about: just a site to see while enjoying a break.

The place sedates me and I become extremely relaxed. Then, all at once, all of my innermost thoughts seek, no, they *require* a note pad, ink pen or pencil, okay and a pocket dictionary. I've been procrastinating about writing this story. It's a story about a man I have never met. I know where he lives. He lives in the woods off southbound highway I-295, directly opposite Bolling Air Force Base.

He lives where no other man I've seen lives. I noticed he built his own home, so it fits his living conditions. There is a homemade clothes line, running from tree to tree to hang his clothes on. I noticed when the weather conditions are unbearable, various pieces of plastic cover the home, and bricks are used to reinforce the structure. The home is surrounded by trash. I noticed that the department of sanitation hasn't collected his trash from his yard in years.

Yes, I know this for a fact. I see the yard just about every day in my passing to and from work. I have seen the man only once during my travels. I was traveling home. He looked to be an elderly gentleman. It was hard to tell sitting on a milk crate outside his home. It was a spring day.

And the sun was shining down on him as he stood among fully blossoming trees, flowers, birds flying, and maybe occasionally, once in a while, a dead body left on the side of the roadway.

I often wondered if any police departments ever went to that location for any type of calls for services. A sick person is in need of medical help. I even wondered if, on any occasion, homicide detectives had visited the home to question him about a highway crime. Yet who do you know who would consider climbing over metal guard rails, hurting themselves, to interview a poor old man.

He is human, people; his needs might be our needs. Life is not a one-way street, people. That is why I am more concerned about his health, not so much his mental condition. Good health will give him good peace of mind.

Mentally, or physically, I am probably in his dreams, maybe a hundred times.

He wishes he had a daughter, like me, who cares. And I wish I had my father when he was on the street. I'm writing this story about a person who created his own rent free home, who made a wise choice to live alone. God created the elderly person, and then me, to write this story. I know my father is reading this right about now and is very proud. Knowing his daughter showed interest in a man once like himself.

U Got NBA mail

No Championship Like At Home

This story is about the Washington Wizards. It is about "scoreless players," lost games, tough love, a cheerleader named Dorothy, and a mascot that symbolizes . . . what? All looking for a championship win under the newly announced team name, the Washington Wizards. The team has traveled on many road trips to Kansas, looking for some heart. Some looking for courage, and some oil so they can lubricate their legs for speed. Some players are seeking knowledge. They seek the knowledge of becoming a winner. Some are looking for the Wizards of Oz to speak out in a roaring voice.

Maybe some like to wait for an inflamed basketball to hit the rim and bounce into the basket. Then step aside and let the other team feel the heat. They went to Kansas to see Oz, and he spoke: "There is a champion in every one of you. Stop whimpering and go win many games. Go home and win." The Wizards needed an extraordinary leader ASAP, a leader that players bend over backwards to play with, that would make them win by any means necessary. They needed to carry out a bull's workout. Not the bull's malt liquor you drink from a can. Players needed a rodeo workout where they would dash up and down the courtside. I guarantee they would learn how to get up and down the court in a timely manner.

The team has some good players; with a lot of hard work, some will become excellent players. Yet, their mindsets drift away into fantasyland, far beyond the rim. The players have no desire to set off a fire in the arena. They get a thrill just watching the fireworks shooting off in the building. Let me introduce myself. I am a fan and attend many losing games. I bring my son to the games and he gets excited when the team is winning. When they start to lose, he directs his attention to me. I keep it real. I stare him straight in the eyes and say, "They're lazy son. The players are playing self-ball." The player whose job is to play forward is playing in the outer perimeter, trying to shoot three-pointers.

What is a center's position? He's supposed to position his body in low post, backing his opponent into the paint, and score.

I do not recall seeing the team's center penalized for a three second violation in years. Okay! Maybe I am lying. I admit being a little disappointed in the team. I do say; I have a notion the Wizards will have a legendary player in the coming years.

And he will have established himself among other players with fame, like Dwight Howard, Amare Stoudemire, Tim Duncan, Yao Ming, Shaquille O'Neal, Rasheed Wallace, Ben Wallace, and David Robinson, as one of the top ten centers in the NBA.

Every player should challenge himself to strive for excellence.

The NBA should hold players accountable for their salaries. It's a billion dollar business, paying for people to play games. There are high school athletes, street ballers, and recreation ball players playing better ball than some NBA players.

All NBA ball players representing our nation's capital, come and show the fans what you are really worth. Everyone could use some free money. Get off those benches and earn your fame. It shouldn't be just about the dollar bills. Have some pride and make a name for yourself. Like LeBron James. I know, I did not go there; forgive me for honesty.

Let's hire players who hunger for a championship.
Hopefully, this year, the owner will hire a new head coach to motivate our potential superstars. Every player, whether in a starting position or off the bench, needs to bring their ace game, or better, to the court. A player who is cool just will not make the cut. Now, with attitude in store, maybe we, the fans, will get to see a losing omen lifted from our team. And a new banner put up for the NBA World Championship winners, the Washington Wizards.

The Sun Showed

Guess what the weather did for me today?

It called me outside to shine down on me.

I looked up at the sky, and the sun had my name on it.

An arrow pierced through it, shaped like a heart.

I started my stroll, head up high, stepping in rhythm, left right, right left,

I smiled with a happy face and made plenty of eye contact through the day.

While walking, I heard car horns blowing. I saw large black crows screaming "hello."

"What a day," and that special one I want to share it with is at work.

No windows in his office to see the sun.

So, I pulled out my Sprint telephone, and called to say "I miss you today."

I didn't care how long I talked, just needed to hear your voice to complete my day.

Ask you to step outside, look up in the sky, and tell me what name the sun is displaying.

Thanks, Mr. Sun, for the adventure today.

A reality I never want to forget. The sun had my name on it.

Twenty-Five Years In The White House

I had to open my eyes back in the 80s. I had heard some shell-shocking news about the treatment of colored officers assigned to the Second District Metropolitan Police Department. The district is located in upper Northwest Washington, D.C., Finally, having graduated from the academy: my newly appointed assignment.

The Second District, permanent midnight shift. It was to be my first day on the job. I opened a door to roll call. White officers sat on one side and black officers on the other side. My mouth dropped wide open. My feet immediately went disabled. They felt glued to floor. A voice said, "Come on in and have a seat."

I hurried myself over to the black section and took a seat. As the weeks came and went, I saw nothing but snow. And, ambiguous as it looked, white ranking officers always masterminded the calls. There were a few token black officials, steered by white officials to keep the other black officers in check, or from going insane. The midnight shift often exposed the white officers' behaviors.

It was certainly an adventure; like rides, amusement parks, race cars, museums, and action figures. Some situations were greater than Wild World. Some situations more exciting than a game board. More flashing than Superman, more mixed than a zebra.

And always controlled by an action figure police officer. I had done my two months on-the-job training and certified to ride alone. The police department classified the term as 1099; one officer to a scout car. Back in the days, the districts where separated into three: Sectors One, Two and Three.

I was assigned to Sector One, Downtown Washington, D.C.; N.W. I covered the area from 14th & Constitution Avenue, N.W., to 22nd and P Street N.W. To district officers, the area was known as the red light district. The geographic make-up consisted of dirty book stores, and ladies of the night. There were transgenders, arcade game rooms, strip clubs, and gay bars.

Like tourists, attracted to the area, people came from everywhere. I saw people, curious and unaware of the areas, festivities being taken for granted. The regular sightseers and doers, knowledgeable about the areas, conquered for pleasure, pain, and partying, and robbed blind, accepted the results.

I met some politicians in the wrong spot. Lost senator, could I be of some aid?

Sometimes, the dispatcher had us respond to calls outside our sector. I can recall a few incidents which occurred in sector two. Sector two covered the Georgetown area. When a citizen called for help, he wanted me to go to the back door, meaning the black door. Then, he asked me to call for a white officer. And like the saying from the movie *Soldier's Story*, "I am all you got." The Metropolitan Police Department sent me here to do my job. I did call for a white official to help. I knew who made the final call.

Now, the moment you all I been waiting for, and without any further introduction, I give you the White House at The Second District. The house was located on the third floor. Most of the officers occupied that floor in a black working capacity, had to be fair colored, meaning light-skinned with their *Emancipation Proclamation* papers.

Then, it was the Underground Railroad, a floor below, occupied by majority black officers (station crew), dealing with the everyday situations and added stress coming from the White House.

Humor in the house was like a breath of fresh air to black officers. I often visited the grounds to watch the black officers do an old folks stomping dance. When a radio call or a telephone call came from the White House, it set the mode for black officers. The officers immediately went into joke mode.

They would say, "I am coming master."

"Let me see you do the dance."

"Do you have your papers?"

"You a shade bit too dark, outer here."

Some officers could do that dance. The dance was an old folk ritual. The dance's moves were to extend both arms forward. Then our palms outward and a three step stomp moves forward. We then announced, "Here is Sammy, here is Sammy." We would burst out laughing. And tears would fill up in the wells of our eyes. I have retired. I have colleagues working at the White House, even now.

I've now concluded my 25 years of the White House tour. It was the journey that excited me the most, not the destination. I wasn't mistakenly summoned to the White House. I was summoned there so I could witness the behavior of the white people and write this story. I know the word *race* is a running event not a color.. I ran races in elementary school, junior high school, and for the Metropolitan Department back in the 80's.

I ran with people of different colors. I do not recall "on your marks, get set, go," a color. I knew white people were somewhat unsure about people of color. I knew back then, as I know now. Without black people, white people are stagnant.

You Framed Me

I recall a story told by a couple of my co-workers. Both met out for a night on the town. It was football season and a lot of people visit local bars to enjoy games. One peculiar Monday night, they went bar hopping before the game. Both were drunk, but not to the point of being comatose. They watched the Redskins defeat the Dallas Cowboys in overtime.

The men sat around after the game, chatting with people unknown. The men were traveling by way of public transportation, a cab. The men left the Red Roof Bar, located on 15th & Pennsylvania Avenue off E. Street, NW. Both men walked to 17th & Pennsylvania Avenue, NW to flag a cab. They found themselves surrendering to U.S. Secret Services Uniform Agents at gunpoint.

The men were ordered to lie down on the sidewalk. Both men were handcuffed and unlawfully searched. The men inquired into the actions of the agents. The men were told to silence themselves. The agents removed identification from both wallets. The men's names were run through a police data for a records check. No records were found on either man.

The agents said they received an anonymous phone call from a caller describing them as having a weapon. After a while of repeatedly being questioned, the men started to get belligerent. The men kept on the ground and still in handcuff felt uneasy. They knew this was hogwash. The men felt the agent stopped them because they were a salt and pepper team (black and white). The agents needed someone to bother with, to burn time.

The men became frustrated and started questioning the agents. One agent made a racial comment about their friendship. The men questioned the agent's ability to spot a criminal. The name-calling went on, back and forth, between the men and agents. The same agent said, "Let's lock them up. And charge them with being drunk in public and disorderly conduct." Both men were arrested by agents and charged.

The men said, "This is a set-up. We been framed." This is a part of the above story, "Framed."

Vision a Mountain High

I focus on a mountain high. I clear my mind to adventure the ride. Places where I know deep emotions run wild. A knowing atmosphere in which I require a special mate. Places where I know boundaries never come into play.

Places where I know love is open every day. Places visited only by artists, composers and me. To go there, I must take you there. Are you ready to go? Then welcome aboard the mountain high. Now, I must have your full cooperation.

I ask you to take a deep breath and release yourself. Relax your mind and clear the way. I open the window so you can take a deep breath and feel the fresh air penetrate your faces. I will begin our love mountain ride, at no cost.

Fasten your arms tightly around my waist. Close your eyes and slowly moonwalk with both feet in place. Whatever you do, do not free yourself until I command.

I am taking you on a mountain high. Can you feel the windy vibes? Can you feel the fresh breeze that is watering your eyes? Can you feel the windy drift which almost knock us apart? Okay, open your eyes slowly, focus on the picture of a mountain view hanging on the wall. And tell me, "How did you like the mountain vision high?"

Wildest Imagination

I like to meet someone and imagine us as two distance stars.

Coming from two different galaxies. Destiny on coming together to make a start.

Conversation separated only by a large circle. Half, in its form tonight, we finally get to meet.

I am surprised by the moon's forces connected together as one human being. More anxious than ever.

"Don't let the moon fall down on us." Then we grabbed hands and transformed ourselves into natural human beings. We flew among the stars and gazed into each other's sparkling eyes.

A light so bright caused us to see right through each other's clothes. Power we could not control at altitudes so high. I find it breathtaking above the deep clouds in the sky. We read each other's minds, until our thoughts became one. Our feelings became one, not sound, but touch. More precious than forty—year-old bottle of wine cedar kept for a special occasion, our thoughts remained clean. More excited than ever, we were free to fly about the sky. Not bothered by rules or people, we explored our options. We decided to take advantage of the moon for our pleasure.

We approached the circle in its reclined chair shape and boldly hopped aboard, transforming into one being, in order not to fall off.

Like a wild stallion, the moon took off. Within itself, it went through the galaxy's opening holes. We set our eyes on the solar system in its entirety. And dashing through a halo ring pattern with multiple colored lights, so bright our eyes could not stare. Trillions of stars, forming the Little Dipper, the Big Dipper and more exhilarating shapes; suddenly, we became mesmerized, falling to sleep. Awakened by the fall, just too much distance to cover. The moon, transformed into a circle, thrust us off. Yet we experienced all we could on our first date. Maybe I'll imagine a carpet ride to Bethlehem on our second date?

Maybe we can be Jesus and Mary.

And discover the secret that every human being alive is trying to explore.

Whether Mary and Jesus remained pure?

PART 4

Relationships and
Romances

A Lover's Wounds

Your love hurts like a sharp sword pierced slightly into my waist side.

Your love hurts like a bullet wound, an open hole in need of aid.

I'm fortunate these love wounds caused minor injuries, requiring peroxides only.

I'm glad you had a first aid kit from the medicine cabinet.

I'm glad you still loved me enough to render me first aid..

A Hot Vegan

I like eating raw

To feel

Alive

I like raw

It sharpens my brain

It filters my digestive system

I like raw dishes

Soaked in olive oils

Diced raw red peppers, raw yellow onions

And cayenne pepper

These ingredients

Sprinkled all over my salad

And raw vegetables

Warm up my lips

The heat irrepressible

I feel internal love

Coming in to full play

1 am raw, hot, I am hot, I am so hot,
and I want to disclose my raw vegan body for pleasure

A Priceless Triangle

There has been a love triangle going on, right before my eyes.

I have spent time with an individual, now denying me less time.

I have spent time with him, only on his time.

I know countless time is precious and so am I.

So, I hope this love trio info gets all around town.

Tittle-tattle has it; I am in a triangle state of mind.

So, I weep a moment of solid tears.

I need to know where I stand.

I question your plans.

Will you give me more time with you?

So I can appreciate a life of priceless time?

And forgive you for the trio.

You answer, "Yes!"

Now, I will show you how to stop measuring our relationship with a single instrument, a "triangle."

And create for you a heart of art.

I will take the triangle. And break down both sides and make a straight line. Then join the sides together and slide a heart pendant in the middle, which opens inside. Then put a Timex watch running off a Duracell battery inside. And guarantee you a lifetime limited warranty. Do you accept my token of love? And that is why there's nothing more priceless than valuable time spent together.

Avoiding You

Have I been acting odd toward you lately?

Have I been ignoring your sincerity?

Have I been avoiding your worries?

Then forgive me for my unethical display of manners.

I think self-preservation first.

I admit to acting funny at times.

I admit to improving my self-sincerity.

I know worrying builds up stress.

Therefore: I avoid worrying myself.

Years of self-practice is a life lesson.

I am human.

And asking me to venture outside of my comfort zone may cause me unwanted stress.

Yet, teaching serenity lies within my mind, body, and soul.

A gift I acquired from Father.

I need an agreement with voiding. I will not repeat the voids of: acting odd and sincerely ignoring you. I introduce you to your Father who has all the answers to ease your worries.

And when that has been done.

I would have fulfilled the void of *Avoiding You.*

Cured

Stop shaking me.

I know the signs of misuse.

I know you're confused.

I know, I've allowed this behavior.

So, I seek counseling to guide me in the right path.

Guess what? I am rehabilitating myself: I have straightened up my life.

I am not falling short of life, not traveling around in a circle.

I am not going to continue to let you . . . misuse me . . . or confuse my life.

I am cured.

Emotional Feelings

Feelings expressed through anger.

Sometimes feelings express grief and sorrow.

Feelings expressed through body language, and never a sound.

Feelings everybody's sole survivor.

Feelings sometimes mixed emotions.

Journey us to landmarks far beyond our immediate control.

Sometimes drugs, alcohol, and short tempers affect our normal behavior pattern.

Being in control, under these conditions, is abnormal.

Certain outcries of others, is sometimes, uncontrollable.

To feel certain pain for another is human.

Understand why human beings challenge opponents in games like chess or checkers.

Because there are no greater results than when a person wins.

Confined to jail, "It did not stop my mental or physical capacity," said a prisoner.

I had a dream. "I've been to the mountain top," said Martin Luther King.

Maya Angelou wrote, "Why would a caged bird sing, with a fearful trill."

Let's test body, mind, and spirit. Let's be taken over by the hands of the warden or by a hit man. Let's use scissors to take away the bird's flying rights. Under the mentioned circumstances, any person could lose control. See, the hit man succeeded. The bird remained crippled from the clipped wings.

I Admit I'm Scared

Desirable, but I could not touch. That special want, I could not have.

For that need became unbearably long and unsolved.

Then a long distance telephone call. After eight years of not knowing, you felt the same way.

You said, "Coming into town tomorrow, to leave the children here for the summer to play."

"I want to see you before I leave town, hoping we can engage in sexual healing."

I'm scared to say that I want it this way too.

I like being loved and kissed all over my body, in the most sensitive spots. And hugged so tight, until we become stuck like one.

I know that the both of us want this kind of day.

So, if you find my desirable body flopping and resisting your soft, magical fingers and tongue, restraint me and just pick up the telephone receiver, and dial 911.

When someone answers, tell them to send you a medical unit that has a straight jacket to relieve my love-shaking body.

And also, surrender me unconscious with medication, until I fall asleep.

So, when I wake up in the morning, you are home.

Then I can remember your face like the first time we met.

Take for granted *I'm scared* I can still have these feeling after eight years.

Stop Stringing

Me Along

Loose String

Play my love song on your guitar, with only me in mind.

Make sure you tune the strings to develop the sound.

Go on now and sing our song.

A love song from my lyrics, created especially for you.

I do not want you to share with the other women, right now.

Before, I had it sent to Motown, for promotional purposes only.

I know the story involving you and Ms. Missy.

I thought you thought you were stringing me along by the wayside.

I asked you to make sure you service the strings on the guitar.

So, I loosen a string.

To set myself free; no more stringing me on.

I'm gone.

Love

Love is kind.

Love is finding self.

Love is mind.

Love is consuming a fine glass of wine.

These similarities are saying, "love defines loving self."

My Time—Our Time

Last night I heard you cry, but could not find the time, last night. I heard you asked repeatedly for more time, and I asked just the opposite.

I listened as you told me how you want to spend your time with me. But then, I know for sure, you knew that I could not give the time you wanted for.

My career, as the barrier of our time is the one thing I can't yield, for I, also want to achieve and be someone that you could admire and be proud of.

I want you to be patient with me and give me some time. Time not think, but time for me to mend our relationship.

If I could spend all my time with someone, right now, it would be with you.

For a life time.

Never Forgotten

Memories are special and can never be forgotten.

Sometimes events and memories trigger people off.

Sometimes a moment of silence means a big deal.

And sometimes-expressing your deepest thoughts, means the world.

Sometimes questions and answers go unsolved.

Do you love me?

I said, "I love myself."

I practice this method within myself.

I have experienced disappointments in affairs; discomfort, and haven't belonged to them.

I enjoyed your pleasures, happiness, ideas, and disappointments in life.

I did not ask for anything for I already have you who complete my world.

I enjoy your company for you never bore me.

Even when there are times we do not seem to agree in some cases, I still love you and will always love you.

Every ups and down is a learning experience for the both of us.

Yet, knowingly thankful, I will never forget.

No Crime Here

I have shown you how to love. Do you hold me accountable? I have shown you how to surrender yourself to others. Should I be guilty by law? I have shown you the true concepts of caring, sharing, receiving, and believing.

You already had it inside you, just put aside, until I came aboard for the ride. I have shown you my patience, on how to relive a four letter word, "love," in a three-year span. Oh, but time has taken its toll. And time waits for no one.

And time is non-toxic. Yet, time can be classified as deficiency. For time travels during the days, evenings, and nights without sound. So, I fell asleep, during midnight hours, and dreamt about precious time. And I made my final decision to let go. I realized your time outweighed mine. And, like a ship at sea, you need more time to weather the storm.

And there I stood patient, alone; waiting for the moment, the hour, the day, the evening, and night. When I would say these words: "Friend, I do not think I can call you right now. For, I have realized, after all those years, that we've have been on a trip. 'The guilt trip ride.' And neither you, nor I, could ever be guilty for getting off in time."

Safe

The chemistry set the pace, then off to the race: my first date. I had, already, two strikes against my better judgment. First strike is the gambling of monetary funds. Second strike is a true Dallas Cowboys fan since Tom Landry's days. I became leery, thinking one more strike to go. It reminded me of baseball: "Three strikes, you're out of there." Our first date, as it relates to strike number two, was to take place inside a club named Nellie's.

It was the rival game between the Washington Redskins and the Dallas Cowboys. The Redskins were trying to clinch a wild card spot in the playoffs. Remember, I had one more strike before I was out.

I figured if the Redskins lost, that's three strikes.I had no solid plan on how to get my team to win, except a validation pass from Joe Gibbs.

Why not use my last resource. So I called my youngest sister in Fort Worth Dallas, Texas, and requested a giant act of kindness. I gave her the complimentary number off the pass. I explained to my sister that Tony Romo is in love with Jessica Sims. So, when she is not at a game, he loses himself and the game.

I arrived early at the club and stayed stationary inside my truck. Listening to love lyrics, knowing, in just minutes, he would arrive.

When he approached the passenger door, shirt wide open and nothing showing but chest, I concentrated solely on his muscle protruding outside the shirt.

I did not share the disclosure until we arrived inside the bar and went upstairs onto a barstool.

I took the honor to button up the shirt until it showed little or nothing.

We had good conversation, laughed, clowned around, and shared eye contact strong enough to set off a fire.

The Redskins won the game. I was happy. I remained safe on strike two. Then, outside in the unheated truck, we went to engage in more conversation. I realized there was no need to start the engine for heat. I felt the heat from his body sweating my body. Silence kicked in for a moment, after staring into each other's eyes almost caused my brain to play tricks with my mind.

I had to announce twice for him to leave. Knowing this would be my solution to a cause, before it led to an effect.

We both called it a night in our most passive voices. Then we passed a few kisses, just enough to keep each other's attention. Until we journey on our next date.

Well, it was like driving my Hummer. Everything went uphill. My free pass worked. My charisma kicked in and the Redskins won. Clinch me a spot for another date worth looking forward to.

There's Nothing Wrong with the Line

Back in my school days, I ran track and field. My events were 1500 meter and 4x4 1500-meter relay. I broke my previous record way back then in a 1500 meter, setting a time of 5.23.48. I always revisited Ballou High School's track and field facility to train. My training was strenuous. I ran laps back and forth, up and down the track, for hours. I was in shape. I often sweated from head to toe. My sweat suit was always soaked after workout.

I get into my vehicle and insert a cassette inside the player. I loved "the National Black Anthem," *lift every voice and sing*. I'll roll down all the windows, pop up the sunroof and enjoy the weather. It was raining lightly that day. Yet, I still opened the sunroof to feel the light drops land on my head.

Once home, I made a tall glass of OCOZ supplement. The product contains a C-supplement. I drink it because it restores my immune system.

Then I went upstairs to get my wet sweat suit and change into something more comfortable. I continue my workout regime.

I did ten sets of arm exercises, with ten pound barbells. Once finished, I relax my body. I lie across my bed and turn the lamp switch on. I have a yellow colored light bulb in the lamp. The color gives my room a cozy atmosphere along with relaxation.

I reached down beside my bed for the telephone. I made a call to my baby. Our conversation was flowing well with words. Until I said the word "love." I said, "Do you love me?" A four letter word: l-o-v-e. Suddenly, I heard not a pin drop. I said, in a joking manner, "Is anyone home?"

I repeated myself. I thought maybe he laid the telephone down to go in the bathroom. I wait awhile; no answer. I could not hang up the phone without giving him some more time. I waited another minute, and without hearing any answer I restlessly ended the call.

I wondered if something happened to him while on the line. There were no cell phones back in the day. And I knew, if I paged him, the beeper would continuously beep. So, out of concern for his well-being, I called the operator.

I said, "Operator, operator, this is an emergency. There's something wrong with my baby's number. I am dialing my baby's number and it's busy all time." I asked the operator to see if there was a problem with his line.

The operator replied, "There's no problem with the line. The telephone receiver is off the hook." So, I played our conversation back, over and over in my mind. And I lay across my bed in disbelief. Then, suddenly, it came to mind.

When I mentioned the word "love," he gets stupefied. And he often silences the phone over the word "love." I will give him a chance to call me back. He always calls back. I'm glad I did not hang up right away. I'm glad the operator had good news about the telephone line.

My words had power, which shouted his mouth closed. I am not apologizing for using a positive word. I love connecting. Thanks again operator, for checking the line.

Through The Years

Through the years, I've met several people and shed some tears. And then you came along and dried my eyes crystal clear. You excited me, enticed me, entrusted me, exhausted me, and befriended me. Since I met you, you were always had been my scenery. You whispered sweet words like music playing in my ears.

I've found heaven right down here on Earth. My search is over. Then right up to the altar, hand in hand. Togetherness was all I've ever wanted. Within years, time got better. Suddenly, I couldn't find one reason to shed a tear.

Then, I received a telephone call one evening. The caller said "Hello" in a sweet voice. I listened and never made a sound. I hung up the telephone, when a voice in my head said, "Here you go again! Here you go again!"

I thought, "Here goes my heartache again." How can I continue the year knowing the shocking news? So, I closed my eyes, said a prayer, and woke up the next morning, eyes crystal clear.

I believe time will heal all pain. And somewhat bothered by the voice in my ears. They whisper as if they are telling me to do unnecessary things. Yet, no disappointment for the way I feel. This is why I've dismissed you, dear. Thanks for the years.

Valentine Passion

Will you be my Valentine?

I said, in a gentle manner, "Can you go out with me?"

I felt unease to ask you for such a special night.

I asked, knowingly, after feeling an impulse from each our hearts.

So, to get a possible date, I used a pickup line straight from the heart.

I said, "Roses are red, violets blue; a beautiful face like yours should belong to me."

Will you be my Valentine's date?

You're Really Missed

I rush home from work, the dentist, and the store, to find that you're not coming home.

I feel a sense of loneliness inside and my body's tingling.

Sweats in my face race swiftly as one drop from other touches the ground and straight to my body.

I feel the cold sweat running through my body.

I feel my heart beating faster than normal and hear it thump like a drum.

I sit down in my reclined chair to slow down.

I turn on the radio station.

I listen to the quiet storm to ease my mind.

I woke up in the morning with doubts lingering in my mind.

I heard a moment of doubt in your voice.

Letting me know this is good bye

When you left with a smile on your face,

I knew right away that you are not coming home.

I shed some tears; then wiped my eyes clear.

I knew, one day, my mistakes would cause this day. Yet, I cherished the good times we spent together throughout the year.

I will always keep a special place in my heart for you.

And value our previous times together.

I know, not communicating with each other caused this separation.

So, if by chance, we meet again. I will talk non-stop. Until you take your lips and press gently against my lips and shut me up. If, by chance we meet again. *You're really missed* are the words I wanted to say to you until the day we meet again.

About the Author

Linda M. Washington, a native Washingtonian, retired from the Metropolitan Police Department after twenty-five years of service. She works now as a court security officer in the Washington D.C. area with the District of Columbia Superior Court. Ms. Washington is a newcomer to the life of publishing. This will be her first book, titled *Eye Unlocked*.

She has written and published a few poems in the Fraternal Orders of Police Simulcast newspaper, back in the 90s. She wrote a poem titled, "Love, Help and Hate." The poem was sent to Nashville, Tennessee; a demo record was made, inspired by the poem. She was a semifinalist in the International Open Poetry Contest for her submission, titled "No Crime Here." She designed all of the artwork throughout the book. Her plans involve a move to Dallas-Fort Worth, Texas, an area close to her sisters, while continuing to pursue her career in writing and illustration.